Giving a F*ck: For a Better World

Somdip Dey

Published by Somdip Dey, 2023.

GIVING A F*CK: FOR A BETTER WORLD

First edition. April 13, 2023.

ISBN: 979-8215336397

Written by Somdip Dey.

About the author

Somdip Dey, FRSA

SOMDIP DEY, FRSA, ALSO professionally known as InteliDey, is an Embedded Artificial Intelligence scientist, engineer, entrepreneur, AI art & music creator and TED speaker. Dey is the CEO of Nosh Technologies, the CTO of Blockway Technologies and a Lecturer at the University of Essex, UK. He is also the Danah Zohar Professor of Quantum Philosophy & Professor of Practice (AI/ML) at Woxsen University, India. He has more than 13 years of industrial experience including working for Microsoft and Samsung in developing numerous technological products that are currently used by billions of people in different ways. For contributions to improving society through applications of embedded machine learning Dey is elected a Life Fellow of the Royal Society of Arts, named an MIT Innovator Under 35, an Outstanding Achiever in Education, Science & Innovation at the 2023 India UK Achievers Honours and a 2022 World IP Review Leader. He is also a member of the Forbes Technology Council and regularly appears in news including Forbes, Entrepreneur, Business Insider, Tech Crunch and many more.

Prologue

Welcome to "Giving a F*ck," a book that aims to raise awareness of some of the most pressing world problems we face today. As you journey through these pages, you'll discover a wealth of information about the issues that matter most, along with practical steps you can take to make a difference. The goal of this book is not to overwhelm you with the sheer magnitude of these problems, but to empower you to take action in the areas that resonate with you the most.

In this book, you'll find in-depth chapters on twelve major global issues, including climate change, poverty, inequality, global health, food and water insecurity, forced migration and refugee crises, access to education, gender inequality, environmental degradation, political instability and conflict, terrorism and extremism, and cybersecurity and data privacy. Each chapter is filled with useful information, statistics, small steps you can take to help, and technologies you can adopt to make a difference.

We've also included two bonus chapters for entrepreneurs, business leaders, and impact investors. These chapters will help you identify business opportunities related to the mentioned problems, understand how businesses can take action to get involved or help resolve these issues, and learn about the concept of impact investing and its potential to drive positive change.

My personal story of "giving a f*ck" began when I moved to the UK to pursue my master's degree in computer science. In 2014, as I was completing my studies, my parents were involved in a car accident in India that left my mother severely injured and my father paralyzed. I sent all my money back to support their medical treatment, leaving me without enough to buy food for nearly a week. During that time, I resorted to dumpster diving to find food that others had thrown away and survived a week on that.

This first-hand experience of hunger and witnessing the amount of wasted food led me to become actively involved in addressing food waste-related issues. Globally, over 1.3 billion tonnes of food is wasted each year, while more than 690 million people go to bed hungry. Furthermore, food wastage contributes to around 10% of global carbon emissions, making it an environmental issue as well as a social one.

In 2014, my experience with hunger and food waste led me to co-develop the world's first crowd food-sharing platform, called "SHARE.IT." The app enabled users to share their leftovers and surplus food with others in need nearby. By making the app open-source, it has inspired entrepreneurs around the world to adopt similar technologies to reduce food waste. SHARE.IT also won the 3Scale API award at the 2014 Koding's Global Hackathon. That's how I started my crusade against food waste and hunger.

As you read this book, remember that you don't have to "give a f*ck" about every problem mentioned here. Instead, we encourage you to choose one or more problems close to your heart and use the information and tools provided in these pages to make a difference in the world. Every small step counts, and together, we can create a more sustainable, equitable, and just future for all.

Let's start giving a f*ck today!

Chapter 1: Climate Change - Small Steps, Big Impact

Hello, dear reader! Welcome to the first chapter of "Giving a F*ck." In this chapter, we will dive into the pressing issue of climate change, a challenge that affects every corner of our planet. We'll explore the current state of climate change, discuss small steps you can take to help combat it, and introduce you to technologies that can make a difference. Remember, you don't have to be a superhero to make a change – small actions can have a significant impact.

The Current State of Climate Change

Climate change is an undeniable reality. According to the Intergovernmental Panel on Climate Change (IPCC), the global temperature has risen by approximately 1.2°C (2.2°F) since the pre-industrial era. This increase in temperature is primarily due to human activities, such as the burning of fossil fuels and deforestation, which release vast amounts of greenhouse gases (GHGs) into the atmosphere.

The consequences of climate change are far-reaching and severe. We are already witnessing more frequent and intense extreme weather events, such as heatwaves, droughts, storms, and flooding. Rising sea levels are threatening coastal communities, and ocean acidification is endangering marine ecosystems. Furthermore, climate change is exacerbating global food and water insecurity, forcing people to migrate, and contributing to the loss of biodiversity.

Small Steps to Make a Difference

While it's easy to feel overwhelmed by the magnitude of climate change, there are many small steps you can take to help reduce your carbon footprint and make a positive impact. Here are some suggestions to get you started:

- **Conserve energy**: Making your home more energy-efficient is one of the easiest ways to reduce your carbon footprint. Turn off lights and appliances when not in use, use energy-efficient light bulbs, and unplug electronic devices that draw standby power. Also, consider investing in energy-efficient appliances, as they can save both energy and money in the long run.

- **Reduce, reuse, recycle**: Embrace the three R's to minimize waste and conserve resources. Reduce your consumption of single-use items, reuse products whenever possible, and recycle materials such as paper, plastic, glass, and aluminium. In addition, consider composting your organic waste to reduce the amount of methane-producing garbage that ends up in landfills.
- **Green your commute**: Transportation is a significant source of GHG emissions. To reduce your impact, consider walking, biking, carpooling, or using public transportation instead of driving alone. If you must drive, maintain your vehicle to ensure it runs efficiently, and try to combine trips to reduce the total distance travelled.
- **Eat a planet-friendly diet**: The production of meat, particularly beef, generates a substantial amount of GHGs. By reducing your consumption of meat and dairy products, you can significantly lower your carbon footprint. Opt for plant-based meals, support local and organic farmers, and try to minimize food waste.
- **Be a conscious consumer**: When shopping, consider the environmental impact of the products you purchase. Choose items made from sustainable materials, buy in bulk to reduce packaging waste, and support companies that prioritize eco-friendly practices.

Leveraging Technology to Combat Climate Change

Technology plays a crucial role in addressing climate change, and by adopting and promoting these innovations, you can amplify your impact:

- **Renewable energy**: Solar panels and wind turbines are two popular forms of renewable energy that can help reduce our dependence on fossil fuels. If feasible, consider installing solar panels on your home or supporting community wind projects. Additionally, switch to a utility provider that sources its energy from renewable sources, if available.
- **Energy-efficient technologies**: Smart thermostats, LED lighting, and energy-efficient appliances can all help reduce energy consumption and lower GHG emissions. Upgrading your home with these technologies not only benefits the environment but can also save you money on your energy bills.

- **Electric vehicles (EVs) and hybrids**: Electric and hybrid vehicles emit fewer greenhouse gases and air pollutants than their gasoline-powered counterparts. If you're in the market for a new vehicle, consider purchasing an electric or hybrid model. Additionally, promote the expansion of charging infrastructure in your community by advocating for more EV charging stations.
- **Carbon capture and storage (CCS)**: CCS technology captures CO2 emissions from power plants and industrial processes, preventing them from entering the atmosphere. While this technology is still in its early stages, supporting research and development in this area can help advance its adoption and effectiveness.
- **Plant-based alternatives**: Support companies that produce plant-based alternatives to meat and dairy products. These alternatives often have a smaller carbon footprint, and by choosing them, you can contribute to reducing greenhouse gas

emissions associated with livestock farming.

Raising Awareness and Taking Action

To make a lasting impact in the fight against climate change, it's essential to raise awareness and inspire others to take action. Here are some ways you can get involved and spread the word:

- **Educate yourself and others**: Stay informed about climate change and its consequences, as well as the latest scientific advancements and policy developments. Share this knowledge with your friends, family, and colleagues to help them understand the urgency of the issue and the importance of taking action.
- **Advocate for policy change**: Contact your local, regional, and national representatives to express your concerns about climate change and the need for stronger policies to address it. Encourage them to support legislation that promotes renewable energy, energy efficiency, and emissions reductions.
- **Support organizations**: Many non-profit organizations are working tirelessly to combat climate change. Consider donating your time, money, or expertise to these groups to help amplify their impact.
- **Use your social media influence**: Share articles, videos, and other content related to climate change on your social media platforms. By doing so, you can help raise awareness, engage others in meaningful discussions, and encourage them to take action.
- **Participate in local initiatives**: Join local environmental groups or attend community events focused on sustainability and climate action. Not only will you meet like-minded individuals who share your passion, but you'll also have the opportunity to make a tangible difference in your community.

By taking these small steps and leveraging available technology, you can play a crucial role in the fight against climate change. Remember, every action counts, and together, we can create a more sustainable and resilient world for future generations. In the next chapter, we'll explore another pressing global issue and discuss how you can make a difference. So, keep reading, keep giving a f*ck, and let's change the world together!

Chapter 2: Poverty - Making a Difference One Step at a Time

Welcome back, dear reader! In this chapter, we'll discuss the critical issue of poverty, a problem that affects millions of people worldwide. We'll take a closer look at the current state of poverty, explore small steps you can take to make a difference, and introduce you to technologies that can help alleviate poverty. Remember, every action, no matter how small, can have a positive impact on the lives of those in need.

The Current State of Poverty

Poverty is a global issue that affects people from all walks of life. According to the World Bank, nearly 9.2% of the world's population, or around 689 million people, lived in extreme poverty in 2021, surviving on less than $1.90 per day. While this number has declined significantly in recent decades, the progress has been uneven, and the COVID-19 pandemic has exacerbated the situation, pushing millions more into poverty.

Poverty has far-reaching consequences, including limited access to healthcare, education, and basic amenities like clean water, sanitation, and nutritious food. It also perpetuates the cycle of poverty, as those born into impoverished families often lack the resources and opportunities to escape their circumstances. Inequality further exacerbates poverty, as wealth becomes concentrated among a small percentage of the population, leaving the majority struggling to make ends meet.

Small Steps to Make a Difference

While the issue of poverty may seem insurmountable, there are small steps you can take to help alleviate poverty and improve the lives of those in need:

- **Support local businesses**: By choosing to buy products and services from local businesses, you help create jobs and stimulate economic growth in your community. This, in turn, can help lift people out of poverty.
- **Donate to charities and non-profit organizations**: Many organizations are dedicated to fighting poverty and providing essential services to those in need. Consider donating your time, money, or resources to these organizations to help them make a lasting impact.
- **Advocate for policy changes**: Contact your local, regional, and national representatives and encourage them to support policies that promote economic equality and reduce poverty. This could include policies that address wage gaps, provide social safety nets, and invest in education, healthcare, and infrastructure.
- **Volunteer your time**: Many non-profit organizations rely on volunteers to help carry out their mission. Look for local opportunities to volunteer your time and skills, whether it's serving meals at a homeless shelter, tutoring children, or assisting with job training programs.
- **Raise awareness**: Educate yourself about the causes and consequences of poverty and share this information with friends, family, and colleagues. Use social media to raise awareness and engage others in conversations about poverty and the importance of taking action.

Leveraging Technology to Combat Poverty

Technology plays a vital role in addressing poverty and can be a powerful tool in empowering people and improving their quality of life. By adopting and promoting these technologies, you can help make a difference:

- **Mobile banking and digital finance**: Access to banking

services is often limited in impoverished communities. Mobile banking and digital finance technologies can help bridge this gap, providing people with the means to save money, access loans, and make transactions. By supporting the expansion of these services, you can help promote financial inclusion and empower people to break the cycle of poverty.

- **E-learning platforms**: Access to quality education is a significant barrier for those living in poverty. E-learning platforms can help overcome this obstacle by providing affordable and accessible educational resources for people of all ages. By promoting these platforms and advocating for their adoption, you can help expand educational opportunities for those in need.
- **Telemedicine**: Many impoverished communities lack access to adequate healthcare services. Telemedicine technologies can help bridge this gap by allowing healthcare providers to remotely diagnose, treat, and monitor patients. By supporting the expansion of telemedicine services, you can help improve access to healthcare for those living in poverty.

- **Sustainable agriculture and precision farming**: Technology can play a crucial role in increasing agricultural productivity and ensuring food security for impoverished communities. Sustainable agriculture practices and precision farming technologies, such as the use of drones and sensors, can help farmers optimize their resources and maximize crop yields. By promoting the adoption of these technologies, you can contribute to alleviating hunger and poverty.
- **Renewable energy and energy-efficient technologies**: Access to affordable and reliable energy is essential for reducing poverty and improving living standards. By supporting the adoption of renewable energy sources and energy-efficient

technologies, you can help provide clean, affordable energy to those in need, while also addressing the issue of climate change.

Raising Awareness and Taking Action

Just like with climate change, raising awareness about poverty and its consequences is essential to inspire others to take action. Here are some ways you can get involved and spread the word:

- **Share personal stories**: By sharing the stories of those affected by poverty, you can humanize the issue and create empathy among others. Use your social media platforms, blog, or local community events to share these stories and bring attention to the challenges faced by those living in poverty.
- **Organize or participate in fundraising events**: Fundraising events, such as charity runs, bake sales, or auctions, can raise money for organizations working to combat poverty while also raising awareness about the issue. Consider organizing or participating in such events to support poverty alleviation efforts.
- **Partner with local schools and educational institutions**: Collaborate with schools and educational institutions to raise awareness about poverty and its consequences. This could involve organizing workshops, presentations, or panel discussions, and providing educational resources for students and teachers.
- **Engage with your community**: Reach out to your community and engage them in conversations about poverty and its impact on society. Encourage your community to take action by volunteering, donating, or advocating for policy changes.

By taking these small steps and leveraging available technology, you can play a vital role in the fight against poverty. Remember, every action counts, and together, we can create a more equitable and prosperous world for all. In the next chapter, we'll explore another pressing global issue and discuss how you can make a difference. So, keep reading, keep giving a f*ck, and let's change the world together!

Chapter 3: Inequality - Bridging the Gap and Harnessing Technology for a Fairer World

Hey there, welcome back to "Giving a F*ck"! We've already covered climate change and poverty, and now it's time to tackle another critical issue: inequality. In this chapter, we'll dive into the different forms of inequality, provide some statistical insights, and discuss the small steps we can take to help address this pervasive problem. We'll also explore some of the amazing technologies that are available to help level the playing field and promote a more equitable society.

Inequality comes in many forms, from income and wealth disparities to disparities in education, healthcare, and opportunities. It affects people of all backgrounds and can perpetuate cycles of poverty and disadvantage. Let's take a look at some of the statistics that illustrate the scale of this problem:

- According to the World Bank, the global Gini coefficient, a measure of income inequality, was 0.63 in 2021. A Gini coefficient of 0 represents perfect equality, while a coefficient of 1 represents perfect inequality.
- The World Inequality Report 2021 found that the top 1% of the global population held 33% of the world's wealth, while the bottom 50% held just 2%.
- Data from the World Economic Forum indicates that the global gender pay gap stood at 16% in 2021, with women earning, on average, 84 cents for every dollar earned by men.

These numbers are certainly sobering, but remember, we're here to talk about solutions, not dwell on the problem. So, let's discuss some small steps you can take to help address inequality in your own life and community.

Small Steps to Make a Difference

- **Promote equal opportunities**: Advocate for policies and practices that ensure equal opportunities for all, regardless of gender, race, ethnicity, or socio-economic background. This could include supporting initiatives to close the gender pay gap, increase diversity in the workplace, or provide equal access to education and training opportunities.
- **Mentor and support others**: Offer your time and expertise to mentor individuals from underrepresented or disadvantaged backgrounds. This could involve volunteering with local youth organizations, participating in mentorship programs, or simply offering guidance and support to those in your network who could benefit from your experience.
- **Support local businesses**: Help reduce income inequality by supporting local businesses and cooperatives, particularly those owned and operated by individuals from marginalized communities. This can help create jobs, build wealth, and promote economic empowerment.
- **Be an ally**: Listen, learn, and stand up against discrimination and prejudice when you encounter it. Educate yourself about the experiences of others and use your voice to advocate for change.

Now that we've covered some personal actions, let's take a look at some of the innovative technologies that are helping to reduce inequality.

Technologies to Combat Inequality

- **Artificial intelligence and machine learning**: While AI and machine learning have the potential to exacerbate inequality, they can also be powerful tools in the fight against it. For example, AI-driven recruitment platforms can help minimize bias in the hiring process, while machine learning algorithms can be used to identify and address patterns of discrimination in areas like housing, lending, and education.

- **Online learning and educational technology**: As we mentioned in the previous chapter, e-learning platforms can help bridge the education gap and provide access to quality learning resources for all, regardless of income or location. Support the development and adoption of these technologies to help ensure that everyone has an equal opportunity to learn and grow.
- **Telecommuting and remote work tools**: Remote work has the potential to reduce income inequality by providing access to better-paying job opportunities for those living in economically disadvantaged areas. By promoting the adoption of remote work tools and supporting policies that encourage flexible work arrangements, we can help create more inclusive and diverse workforces.

- **Blockchain technology**: Blockchain can promote greater transparency and reduce corruption by creating tamper-proof, decentralized records. This technology has the potential to address issues such as land rights disputes, voting fraud, and supply chain exploitation, all of which contribute to inequality.
- **Accessible technology for people with disabilities**: Assistive technologies, such as screen readers, speech-to-text software, and mobility devices, can help level the playing field for people with disabilities, ensuring they have equal opportunities to participate in society. Support the development and adoption of these technologies to promote a more inclusive world.

Raising Awareness and Taking Action

As with the previous chapters, one of the most powerful tools at your disposal is your voice. Talk to your friends, family, and colleagues about inequality and the steps we can take to address it. Share information on social media, attend local events, and join advocacy groups to stay informed and engaged. By raising awareness, you can inspire others to take action and help build momentum for policies and initiatives that promote equality and justice.

In this chapter, we've explored some of the small steps you can take and the innovative technologies available to help combat inequality. Remember, every action counts, and your contributions – no matter how small – can make a real difference in the lives of others.

Stay tuned for the next chapter of "Giving a F*ck," *where we'll tackle another pressing issue and discuss how we can work together to create positive change. Keep learning, keep sharing, and never stop giving a f*ck*! Together, we can make a meaningful impact and build a more just, equitable, and inclusive world for all.

Chapter 4: Global Health Issues - Nurturing a Healthier World One Step at a Time

Hello again and welcome back to "Giving a F*ck"! We've covered climate change, poverty, and inequality so far, and now we're ready to dive into another crucial topic: global health issues. In this chapter, we'll take a closer look at some of the most pressing health challenges facing our world today, provide statistical insights, and discuss the small steps we can take to make a difference. Additionally, we'll explore some of the innovative technologies available to help address these issues and how you can adopt them to raise awareness and contribute to global health solutions.

Global health issues are complex and interconnected, affecting billions of people across the planet. From infectious diseases and malnutrition to mental health and non-communicable diseases, these challenges can have profound consequences for individuals, communities, and entire nations. Let's examine some statistics that highlight the scale and urgency of global health issues:

- The World Health Organization (WHO) reports that approximately 9.6 million people died of cancer in 2018, making it the second leading cause of death globally.
- According to the United Nations, nearly 690 million people suffered from chronic undernourishment in 2019, and an estimated 144 million children under the age of 5 were affected by stunting due to malnutrition.
- The WHO states that, as of 2021, more than 1.13 billion people worldwide suffer from hypertension, a major risk factor for heart disease and stroke.
- Mental health disorders affect hundreds of millions of people globally. The WHO estimates that around 264 million people

suffer from depression, and close to 800,000 people die due to suicide every year.

While these numbers can be overwhelming, it's important to remember that we all have the power to make a difference, even through seemingly small actions. So, let's discuss some steps you can take to help address global health issues and contribute to a healthier world.

Small Steps to Make a Difference

- **Educate yourself and others**: Knowledge is power, and understanding the complexities of global health issues is essential for finding effective solutions. Stay informed about the latest developments, share your knowledge with others, and engage in conversations to raise awareness about these critical challenges.
- **Support health-focused organizations**: Donate to reputable organizations that are working to address global health issues, such as the WHO, UNICEF, or Doctors Without Borders. Even modest contributions can have a significant impact on the lives of those in need.
- **Adopt healthy habits**: Taking care of your own health is an important step in contributing to global health. Adopt healthy habits, such as eating a balanced diet, exercising regularly, getting enough sleep, and managing stress. Encourage your friends and family to do the same.
- **Advocate for change**: Use your voice to advocate for policies and initiatives that promote health and well-being at the local, national, and global levels. This might include supporting efforts to increase access to healthcare, improve public health infrastructure, or address the social determinants of health.

Now that we've covered some personal actions, let's explore some of the ground-breaking technologies that are helping to address global health issues.

Technologies to Combat Global Health Issues

- **Telemedicine**: As we mentioned in the chapter on poverty, telemedicine platforms are revolutionizing access to healthcare for millions of people around the world. By connecting patients with healthcare providers remotely, these platforms help bridge the gap in access to quality care, particularly in underserved or remote communities.
- **Mobile health (mHealth) applications**: Mobile health apps, such as MyFitnessPal, Headspace, and Ada, are empowering individuals to take control of their health and well-being. These apps can help users monitor their nutrition, track exercise, manage stress, and even receive personalized health advice. By supporting the development and adoption of these technologies, we can help promote healthier lifestyles and better self-care habits.

- **Artificial intelligence (AI) in diagnostics and treatment**: AI and machine learning are transforming the way we diagnose and treat diseases. From analyzing medical images to predicting disease outbreaks, AI-driven tools are enabling healthcare providers to make more accurate and timely decisions, ultimately improving patient outcomes.
- **Vaccine development technologies**: Rapid advances in vaccine development technologies, such as mRNA platforms, have demonstrated their potential to address infectious diseases more effectively. By supporting the research and development of these technologies, we can help protect populations from existing and emerging diseases.

- **Wearable health devices:** Wearable technologies like fitness trackers, smartwatches, and heart rate monitors are not only helping individuals monitor and manage their health but also providing valuable data for researchers and healthcare providers. The widespread adoption of these devices has the potential to revolutionize the way we approach preventative care and early intervention.

Raising Awareness and Taking Action

As with the other chapters, your voice is an invaluable tool in raising awareness and inspiring action. Share information about global health issues and the innovative technologies available to address them with your friends, family, and colleagues. Engage in conversations, attend local events, and join advocacy groups to stay informed and involved. By raising awareness, you can help build momentum for policies and initiatives that promote health and well-being for all.

In this chapter, we've explored some of the small steps you can take and the innovative technologies available to help address global health issues. Remember, every action counts, and your contributions – no matter how small – can make a real difference in the lives of others.

Stay tuned for the next chapter of "Giving a F*ck," *where we'll tackle another pressing issue and discuss how we can work together to create positive change. Keep learning, keep sharing, and never stop giving a f*ck*! Together, we can make a meaningful impact and build a healthier, more resilient world for everyone.

Chapter 5: Food and Water Insecurity - Sowing the Seeds of Change for a Nourished and Hydrated World

Welcome back to "Giving a F*ck"! We've already discussed climate change, poverty, inequality, and global health issues, and now it's time to focus on another critical challenge: food and water insecurity. In this chapter, we'll explore the causes and consequences of food and water insecurity, delve into some pertinent statistics, and discuss the small steps we can take to help address this problem. We'll also examine the innovative technologies that are available to help combat food and water insecurity and explore how you can adopt these solutions to raise awareness and contribute to a more secure and sustainable future.

Food and water insecurity are closely intertwined and affect billions of people worldwide. From droughts and floods to conflicts and economic crises, a variety of factors can disrupt access to these essential resources, leading to malnutrition, illness, and even death. Let's take a look at some statistics that underscore the scale of the problem:

- According to the United Nations, nearly 690 million people suffered from hunger in 2019, and an estimated 3 billion people could not afford a healthy diet.
- The World Health Organization (WHO) reports that approximately 2.2 billion people lacked access to safely managed drinking water services in 2021.
- The United Nations estimates that by 2025, two-thirds of the global population could be living under water-stressed conditions, with 1.8 billion people experiencing absolute water scarcity.

These figures are undoubtedly alarming, but remember, our goal here is to focus on solutions, not to dwell on the problem. So, let's talk about some small steps you can take to help address food and water insecurity and contribute to a more sustainable and secure future.

Small Steps to Make a Difference

- **Reduce food waste**: An astonishing one-third of all food produced worldwide is wasted. By planning meals carefully, storing food properly, and repurposing leftovers, you can help reduce food waste and make a positive impact on global food security.
- **Conserve water**: Adopt water-saving habits, such as fixing leaks, installing water-efficient appliances, and using a rain barrel to collect water for your garden. These actions may seem small, but collectively they can make a significant difference in conserving our precious water resources.
- **Support sustainable agriculture**: Choose locally-produced, sustainably-sourced food products whenever possible. By supporting farmers who practice environmentally responsible agriculture, you can help promote a more sustainable and secure food system.
- **Raise awareness and advocate for change**: Use your voice to raise awareness about food and water insecurity, and advocate for policies and initiatives that promote sustainable resource management and equitable access to food and water.

Now that we've covered some personal actions, let's take a look at some of the cutting-edge technologies that are helping to address food and water insecurity.

Technologies to Combat Food and Water Insecurity

- **Precision agriculture**: Precision agriculture technologies, such as satellite imagery, drones, and sensors, enable farmers to optimize their use of resources like water, fertilizers, and pesticides, resulting in more efficient and sustainable agricultural practices. By supporting the adoption of these technologies, we can help improve crop yields and reduce the environmental impact of agriculture.

- **Vertical farming and hydroponics**: Vertical farming and hydroponic systems allow for the cultivation of crops in controlled environments, using significantly less water and land than traditional farming methods. These innovative techniques have the potential to increase food production in urban areas and contribute to global food security.
- **Solar-powered water purification**: Solar-powered water purification systems, such as solar stills and solar-powered reverse osmosis units, offer a sustainable solution for providing clean drinking water in remote or off-grid communities. By supporting the development and deployment of these technologies, we can help improve access to clean water for millions of people around the world.

- **Biotechnology and genetically modified organisms (GMOs)**: Biotechnology advancements, including genetically modified crops, can help address food insecurity by developing plants that are more resistant to diseases, pests, and environmental stressors like drought. While GMOs remain a controversial topic, supporting responsible research and development in this field can contribute to more resilient and productive food systems.
- **Water management and monitoring technologies**: Smart water management systems, such as IoT-enabled sensors and data analytics tools, can help optimize water use and reduce waste in agricultural, industrial, and residential settings. As a

consumer you can use the Nosh app to better manage food at home and optimize food waste through in-app intelligent analytics and shopping planning. If you have food surplus, then you can use OLIO to share the surplus with other people nearby who might want it. To get discounted food that are about-to-be-thrown-away from shops and restaurants then another option is to use the Too Good To Go app for the purpose. By promoting the adoption of these technologies, we can contribute to more efficient and sustainable water management practices.

Raising Awareness and Taking Action

As in the previous chapters, your voice is a powerful tool for raising awareness and inspiring action. Share information about food and water insecurity and the innovative technologies available to address these challenges with your friends, family, and colleagues. Engage in conversations, attend local events, and join advocacy groups to stay informed and involved. By raising awareness, you can help build momentum for policies and initiatives that promote sustainable resource management and equitable access to food and water.

In this chapter, we've explored some of the small steps you can take and the innovative technologies available to help address food and water insecurity. Remember, every action counts, and your contributions – no matter how small – can make a real difference in the lives of others.

Stay tuned for the next chapter of "Giving a F*ck," *where we'll tackle another pressing issue and discuss how we can work together to create positive change. Keep learning, keep sharing, and never stop giving a f*ck*! Together, we can make a meaningful impact and build a more secure, sustainable, and nourished world for all.

Chapter 6: Forced Migration and Refugee Crises - Extending a Helping Hand to Those in Need

Welcome back to "Giving a F*ck"! In previous chapters, we've tackled climate change, poverty, inequality, global health issues, and food and water insecurity. Now it's time to focus on another critical challenge facing our world today: forced migration and refugee crises. In this chapter, we'll explore the causes and consequences of forced migration, provide statistical insights, and discuss the small steps we can take to help address this issue. We'll also look at some of the innovative technologies that are available to assist refugees and migrants, and explore how you can adopt these solutions to raise awareness and contribute to a more compassionate and supportive world.

Forced migration refers to the movement of people from their homes due to factors such as conflict, persecution, natural disasters, or environmental degradation. The consequences of forced migration can be devastating, leading to loss of life, trauma, and long-term displacement for millions of people around the world. Let's examine some statistics that highlight the scale and urgency of this issue:

- According to the United Nations High Commissioner for Refugees (UNHCR), by the end of 2020, there were 82.4 million forcibly displaced people worldwide, including 26.4 million refugees, 48 million internally displaced persons, and 4.1 million asylum-seekers.
- The UNHCR also reports that nearly 1% of the world's population is now forcibly displaced, with 23,800 people being forced to flee their homes every day.
- A staggering 42% of all refugees are children under the age of 18, according to UNHCR data.

While these figures can be disheartening, it's important to remember that we all have the power to make a difference, even through seemingly small actions. So, let's discuss some steps you can take to help address forced migration and refugee crises and contribute to a more compassionate and supportive world.

Small Steps to Make a Difference

- **Educate yourself and others**: Understanding the complexities of forced migration is essential for finding effective solutions. Stay informed about the latest developments, share your knowledge with others, and engage in conversations to raise awareness about this critical issue.
- **Donate to reputable organizations**: Support organizations that are working to address the needs of refugees and forcibly displaced persons, such as UNHCR, International Rescue Committee, or Save the Children. Your contributions can make a significant impact on the lives of those in need.
- **Volunteer your time and skills**: Many organizations assisting refugees and migrants require volunteers to help with various tasks, such as language tutoring, legal assistance, or fundraising. Offering your time and skills can make a meaningful difference in the lives of those affected by forced migration.
- **Advocate for change**: Use your voice to advocate for policies and initiatives that support refugees and forcibly displaced persons. This might include supporting efforts to increase access to education, healthcare, and employment opportunities, as well as promoting policies that uphold the human rights of all individuals, regardless of their migration status.

Now that we've covered some personal actions, let's explore some of the ground-breaking technologies that are helping to address forced migration and refugee crises.

Technologies to Assist Refugees and Migrants

- **Mobile applications for refugees**: Mobile apps specifically designed for refugees, such as RefAid, Refugee Aid App, and MigApp, provide crucial information and resources, including location-specific services like medical care, legal assistance, and educational opportunities. By supporting the development and adoption of these technologies, we can help empower refugees and migrants to access essential services and support.
- **Digital identity solutions**: Access to official identification documents is often a significant challenge for refugees and migrants. Digital identity solutions, such as blockchain-based platforms, can provide secure, verifiable, and portable identification for individuals who have been forcibly displaced. By supporting the development and implementation of these technologies, we can help refugees and migrants access essential services and rebuild their lives.

- **Online education platforms**: Education is a critical tool for empowering refugees and migrants and ensuring their long-term success. Online education platforms, such as Coursera for Refugees and Kiron Open Higher Education, offer free access to university-level courses and resources for displaced individuals. Supporting these initiatives can help provide valuable educational opportunities to those who have been forced to leave their homes.
- **Remote mental health support**: The psychological impact of forced migration can be immense, and access to mental health support is often limited. Digital mental health platforms, such as telemedicine apps and chatbots, can provide remote support to refugees and migrants experiencing mental health challenges. By promoting the adoption of these technologies, we can help

improve the well-being of those affected by forced migration.

- **Social media and communication tools**: Social media platforms and communication tools like WhatsApp and Facebook have become vital lifelines for refugees and migrants, enabling them to stay connected with family, access information, and seek support. By supporting the development and accessibility of these tools, we can help ensure that those affected by forced migration can maintain essential connections and access crucial resources.

Raising Awareness and Taking Action

As we've seen throughout this book, your voice is an incredibly powerful tool for raising awareness and inspiring action. Share information about forced migration and refugee crises, as well as the innovative technologies available to help address these challenges, with your friends, family, and colleagues. Engage in conversations, attend local events, and join advocacy groups to stay informed and involved. By raising awareness, you can help build momentum for policies and initiatives that promote compassion, support, and opportunity for refugees and migrants.

In this chapter, we've explored some of the small steps you can take and the innovative technologies available to help address forced migration and refugee crises. Remember, every action counts, and your contributions – no matter how small – can make a real difference in the lives of others.

Stay tuned for the next chapter of "Giving a F*ck," *where we'll tackle another pressing issue and discuss how we can work together to create positive change. Keep learning, keep sharing, and never stop giving a f*ck*! Together, we can make a meaningful impact and build a more compassionate, supportive, and inclusive world for all.

Chapter 7: Access to Education - Unlocking Opportunities for All

Welcome back to "Giving a F*ck"! So far, we've explored climate change, poverty, inequality, global health issues, food and water insecurity, and forced migration and refugee crises. In this chapter, we'll turn our attention to another critical issue: access to education. We'll provide some statistical insights, discuss the small steps you can take to help address this issue, and explore the innovative technologies available to improve access to education worldwide.

Education is a fundamental human right and a crucial tool for empowering individuals, reducing poverty, and promoting peace and social cohesion. However, millions of children and adults around the world continue to face barriers to accessing quality education. Let's take a look at some statistics that highlight the scope and severity of this issue:

- According to UNESCO, in 2021, 258 million children, adolescents, and youth were out of school worldwide.
- The World Bank estimates that 53% of children in low- and middle-income countries cannot read and understand a simple story by the end of primary school.
- Girls are particularly affected by a lack of access to education: UNESCO data indicates that, in 2021, 130 million girls between the ages of 6 and 17 were out of school, and 15 million girls of primary school age will never have the opportunity to learn to read or write in primary school.

These statistics are sobering, but as we've learned throughout this book, even small actions can make a significant difference. So, let's explore some steps you can take to help improve access to education for all.

Small Steps to Make a Difference

- **Educate yourself and others**: Stay informed about the latest developments and challenges related to access to education, both locally and globally. Share your knowledge with others and engage in conversations to raise awareness about this critical issue.
- **Support education-focused organizations**: Donate to reputable organizations that work to improve access to education, such as Room to Read, UNICEF, or Save the Children. Your financial support can help fund essential educational programs and initiatives for children and adults in need.
- **Volunteer your time and skills**: Many organizations require volunteers to help with tutoring, mentoring, or teaching. Offer your time and expertise to assist students in your local community or support global education initiatives through remote volunteering opportunities.
- **Advocate for change**: Use your voice to advocate for policies and initiatives that promote equal access to quality education for all. This might include supporting efforts to increase funding for public education, reduce barriers to education for marginalized populations, or promote inclusive and equitable educational practices.

Now that we've covered some personal actions, let's take a look at some of the innovative technologies that are helping to improve access to education worldwide.

Technologies to Improve Access to Education

- **Online learning platforms**: Digital learning platforms, such as Khan Academy, Coursera, and edX, offer free or low-cost access to a wide range of educational resources, including video lectures, interactive exercises, and assessments. By promoting the adoption and accessibility of these platforms, we can help ensure that learners from all backgrounds have the opportunity to access quality education.

- **Mobile applications for education**: Mobile apps, such as Duolingo, Quizlet, and Photomath, provide engaging and interactive educational content that can be accessed on the go. By supporting the development and use of these apps, we can help make education more accessible and enjoyable for learners around the world.
- **E-readers and digital libraries**: E-readers and digital libraries, such as Worldreader and Project Gutenberg, offer access to thousands of books and educational materials, often at no cost. These resources can be particularly valuable for learners in remote or underserved areas where access to physical books and learning materials may be limited. By promoting the use of e-readers and digital libraries, we can help break down barriers to education and promote a love of learning.

- **Virtual reality (VR) and augmented reality (AR) in education**: VR and AR technologies have the potential to revolutionize education by offering immersive, interactive, and engaging learning experiences. For example, VR can transport students to historical sites or allow them to explore complex scientific concepts in a hands-on way. By supporting the development and implementation of these technologies, we can help transform education and make it more accessible and engaging for all learners.
- **Artificial intelligence (AI) and personalized learning**: AI-driven education platforms, such as Carnegie Learning and DreamBox, use machine learning algorithms to provide

personalized learning experiences tailored to each student's unique needs and abilities. By promoting the adoption of AI-driven education solutions, we can help ensure that every learner receives the support and resources they need to succeed.

Raising Awareness and Taking Action

As with other issues we've discussed in this book, raising awareness about the importance of access to education is critical. Share information about the challenges and opportunities related to education, as well as the innovative technologies available to help address these issues, with your friends, family, and colleagues. Engage in conversations, attend local events, and join advocacy groups to stay informed and involved.

By raising awareness and taking small actions, you can contribute to the global effort to ensure that every child and adult has the opportunity to access quality education. In the next chapter of "Giving a F*ck," *we'll explore another pressing issue and discuss how we can work together to create positive change. Keep learning, keep sharing, and never stop giving a f*ck*! Together, we can make a meaningful impact and build a more just, equitable, and educated world for all.

Chapter 8: Gender Inequality - Breaking Down Barriers and Empowering Everyone

Welcome back to "Giving a F*ck"! We've already covered several pressing global issues, including climate change, poverty, inequality, global health issues, food and water insecurity, forced migration and refugee crises, and access to education. In this chapter, we'll tackle another vital issue: gender inequality. We'll provide statistical insights, explore the small steps you can take to help address this issue, and discuss the innovative technologies available to promote gender equality worldwide.

Gender inequality is a complex and pervasive issue that affects individuals and societies around the world. It manifests in various ways, such as disparities in income, access to education and healthcare, and opportunities for career advancement. Let's take a look at some statistics that highlight the scope and severity of gender inequality:

- According to the World Economic Forum's Global Gender Gap Report 2020, at the current rate of progress, it will take another 99.5 years to achieve gender parity.
- UNICEF data shows that, globally, girls are less likely than boys to attend primary school, with 9% of primary-school-aged girls out of school compared to 6% of boys.
- The International Labour Organization (ILO) estimates that the global gender pay gap stands at approximately 20%, with women earning on average 80 cents for every dollar earned by men.

These statistics are disheartening, but as we've learned throughout this book, even small actions can make a significant difference. So, let's explore some steps you can take to help improve gender equality.

Small Steps to Make a Difference

- **Educate yourself and others**: Learn about the various aspects of gender inequality, both locally and globally, and share your knowledge with others. Engage in conversations and debates to raise awareness and foster understanding about this critical issue.
- **Support gender equality-focused organizations**: Donate to reputable organizations that work to promote gender equality, such as UN Women, Girls Not Brides, or Malala Fund. Your financial support can help fund essential programs and initiatives that empower women and girls around the world.
- **Challenge stereotypes and biases**: Recognize and challenge gender stereotypes and biases in your own thoughts and actions, as well as those of others. Encourage open dialogue and promote the idea that everyone should be free to pursue their goals and dreams, regardless of their gender.
- **Advocate for change**: Use your voice to advocate for policies and initiatives that promote gender equality, such as equal pay for equal work, paid parental leave, and stronger protections against gender-based violence. Support efforts to increase representation and inclusion of women and gender minorities in leadership roles and decision-making processes.

Now that we've covered some personal actions, let's take a look at some of the innovative technologies that are helping to promote gender equality worldwide.

Technologies to Promote Gender Equality

- **Mobile apps for women's safety**: Personal safety apps, such as Circle of 6, SafeTrek, and Hollaback!, provide tools and resources for women and other vulnerable populations to seek help in unsafe situations. By supporting the development and use of these apps, we can help create safer environments for everyone.

- **Digital financial services for women**: Access to financial services is crucial for women's empowerment and economic independence. Mobile banking and digital finance apps, such as Tala, M-Pesa, and Grameen Bank, offer convenient and accessible financial services to women, particularly in underserved communities. By promoting the adoption of these technologies, we can help empower women financially and foster gender equality.
- **Online education platforms for women**: Digital learning platforms, such as Coursera, edX, and Girl Rising, offer specialized courses and resources aimed at empowering women and girls through education. By promoting the adoption and accessibility of these platforms, we can help ensure that women and girls from all backgrounds have the opportunity to access quality education and develop their skills.

- **Social media and awareness campaigns**: Social media platforms, such as Facebook, Twitter, and Instagram, have the power to amplify voices and raise awareness about gender inequality. By supporting and participating in online campaigns and initiatives, such as #MeToo, #HeForShe, and #GirlsWhoCode, we can help raise awareness and inspire action to promote gender equality.
- **AI-driven tools to combat gender bias**: Artificial intelligence (AI) and machine learning technologies can be utilized to identify and combat gender bias in various contexts, such as hiring practices, performance evaluations, and marketing strategies. Companies like Textio and Blendoor are developing innovative AI-driven solutions to reduce bias and promote

diversity and inclusion in the workplace. By supporting the adoption of these technologies, we can help create more equitable environments for everyone.

Raising Awareness and Taking Action

As with other issues we've discussed in this book, raising awareness about the importance of gender equality is critical. Share information about the challenges and opportunities related to gender inequality, as well as the innovative technologies available to help address these issues, with your friends, family, and colleagues. Engage in conversations, attend local events, and join advocacy groups to stay informed and involved.

By raising awareness and taking small actions, you can contribute to the global effort to ensure that every individual, regardless of their gender, has the opportunity to fulfil their potential and enjoy equal rights and opportunities. In the next chapter of "Giving a F*ck," *we'll explore another pressing issue and discuss how we can work together to create positive change. Keep learning, keep sharing, and never stop giving a f*ck*! Together, we can make a meaningful impact and build a more just, equitable, and inclusive world for all.

Chapter 9: Environmental Degradation - Reversing the Damage and Protecting Our Planet

Welcome back to "Giving a F*ck"! So far, we've tackled various pressing global issues like climate change, poverty, inequality, global health, food and water insecurity, forced migration and refugee crises, access to education, and gender inequality. In this chapter, we'll explore another critical issue: environmental degradation. We'll provide statistical insights, discuss the small steps you can take to help address this issue, and delve into the innovative technologies available to combat environmental degradation.

Environmental degradation refers to the deterioration of the environment through the depletion of natural resources, pollution, habitat destruction, and other factors. Here, "Environmental Degradation" focuses on the broader range of issues related to the deterioration of the natural environment, including habitat destruction, pollution, and loss of biodiversity. On the other hand, "Climate Change", as we explored in Chapter 1, specifically addresses the long-term shifts in temperature, precipitation patterns, and other atmospheric conditions resulting from human activities, primarily the burning of fossil fuels and deforestation. The issue of environmental degradation affects ecosystems, wildlife, and human populations globally, and its impacts can be both immediate and long-lasting. Let's take a look at some statistics that highlight the scope and severity of environmental degradation:

- According to the World Wildlife Fund (WWF), we've lost approximately half of the world's forests since the beginning of human civilization, and we continue to lose 18.7 million acres of forest annually.

- The World Bank estimates that air pollution causes approximately 4.2 million premature deaths each year.
- The United Nations (UN) reports that biodiversity loss is occurring at an unprecedented rate, with about one million species at risk of extinction due to human activity.

These statistics paint a grim picture, but as we've seen throughout this book, small actions can make a big difference. Let's explore some steps you can take to help mitigate environmental degradation.

Small Steps to Make a Difference

- **Reduce, reuse, recycle**: Practice the three R's to minimize waste and conserve resources. Reduce your consumption of single-use items, reuse products whenever possible, and recycle materials like paper, glass, and plastic.
- **Conserve energy and water**: Turn off lights and appliances when not in use, use energy-efficient bulbs and devices, and unplug chargers to save electricity. Be mindful of your water usage by fixing leaks, taking shorter showers, and using water-saving appliances.
- **Choose sustainable products**: Support companies that prioritize environmental sustainability by choosing products made from eco-friendly materials, produced with minimal waste, and certified by credible environmental organizations.
- **Plant trees and create green spaces**: Trees absorb carbon dioxide, provide habitats for wildlife, and help prevent soil erosion. Planting trees and creating green spaces in your community can help combat deforestation and support local ecosystems.
- **Advocate for environmental policies**: Use your voice to support policies and initiatives that protect the environment, such as renewable energy, waste reduction programs, and

wildlife conservation efforts.

Now that we've covered some personal actions, let's take a look at some of the innovative technologies that are helping to combat environmental degradation worldwide.

Technologies to Combat Environmental Degradation

- **Renewable energy**: Solar, wind, hydroelectric, and other renewable energy sources offer clean alternatives to fossil fuels, reducing greenhouse gas emissions and air pollution. By supporting and adopting renewable energy technologies, we can help combat climate change and minimize the environmental impacts of energy production.
- **Water-saving technologies**: Innovations like low-flow faucets, smart irrigation systems, and water-efficient appliances can significantly reduce water consumption. By adopting these water-saving technologies, we can help conserve precious water resources and mitigate the effects of water scarcity.
- **Biodegradable and eco-friendly materials**: Advances in material science have led to the development of biodegradable plastics and other environmentally friendly materials that can help reduce waste and pollution. Supporting and using products made from these materials can help minimize our environmental footprint.
- **Environmental monitoring and data collection**: Remote sensing, satellite imagery, and other advanced data collection technologies allow us to monitor and assess the state of our environment on a global scale. These tools can help us identify areas of concern, track changes over time, and inform conservation efforts. By supporting the development and use of these technologies, we can better understand and address the challenges posed by environmental degradation.

- **Ecosystem restoration technologies**: Techniques such as reforestation, wetland restoration, and coral reef rehabilitation can help reverse environmental degradation and restore damaged ecosystems. By investing in and supporting these restoration technologies, we can contribute to the recovery and preservation of our planet's ecosystems.

Raising Awareness and Taking Action

As with other issues we've discussed in this book, raising awareness about the importance of addressing environmental degradation is crucial. Share information about the challenges and opportunities related to environmental degradation, as well as the innovative technologies available to help address these issues, with your friends, family, and colleagues. Engage in conversations, attend local events, and join advocacy groups to stay informed and involved.

By raising awareness and taking small actions, you can contribute to the global effort to protect our environment and ensure that future generations can enjoy a healthy, thriving planet. In the next chapter of "Giving a F*ck," *we'll explore another pressing issue and discuss how we can work together to create positive change. Keep learning, keep sharing, and never stop giving a f*ck*! Together, we can make a meaningful impact and build a more sustainable and resilient world for all.

Chapter 10: Political Instability and Conflict - Finding Solutions Through Peace and Dialogue

Welcome back to "Giving a F*ck"! We've already covered several pressing global issues, including climate change, poverty, inequality, global health, food and water insecurity, forced migration and refugee crises, access to education, gender inequality, and environmental degradation. In this chapter, we'll explore political instability and conflict – a problem that affects millions of people around the world. We'll provide statistical insights, discuss the small steps you can take to help address this issue, and delve into the innovative technologies available to combat political instability and conflict.

Political instability and conflict occur when disagreements or tensions between nations, groups, or individuals escalate and result in violence or other disruptive actions. These issues can lead to devastating consequences, including loss of life, displacement, economic disruption, and long-lasting societal damage. Here are some statistics that illustrate the scope and severity of political instability and conflict:

- According to the United Nations High Commissioner for Refugees (UNHCR), there were approximately 82.4 million forcibly displaced people worldwide at the end of 2020, primarily due to conflict, persecution, and human rights violations.
- The Institute for Economics and Peace (IEP) estimated that the economic impact of violence in 2020 was $14.96 trillion or roughly 11.6% of the world's GDP.
- The Armed Conflict Location & Event Data Project (ACLED) reported over 110,000 conflict events in 2020, resulting in over 90,000 fatalities.

These statistics are sobering, but there are actions we can take to help reduce political instability and promote peace. Let's explore some steps you can take to help make a difference.

Small Steps to Make a Difference

- **Stay informed and educate others**: Keep up-to-date on current events, learn about the root causes of political instability and conflict, and share this information with others. By promoting understanding and awareness, you can help foster empathy and encourage peaceful resolution of conflicts.
- **Support peacebuilding organizations**: Numerous organizations, such as Peace Direct, Search for Common Ground, and the International Crisis Group, work to prevent, mitigate, and resolve conflicts around the world. By donating to, volunteering for, or advocating on behalf of these organizations, you can help support their vital work.
- **Engage in dialogue and promote tolerance**: Encourage open, respectful conversations with others who hold different views or come from different backgrounds. By fostering dialogue and promoting tolerance, you can help bridge divides and contribute to a more peaceful and inclusive society.
- **Advocate for peaceful policies**: Use your voice to support policies and initiatives that promote diplomacy, dialogue, and non-violent resolution of conflicts. Encourage your political representatives to prioritize peacebuilding efforts and work towards international cooperation.

Now that we've covered some personal actions, let's take a look at some of the innovative technologies that are helping to address political instability and conflict worldwide.

Technologies to Address Political Instability and Conflict

- **Early warning systems**: Advanced data analysis, satellite imagery, and artificial intelligence (AI) can be used to monitor and predict potential conflict hotspots, allowing for early intervention and prevention efforts. By supporting the development and implementation of these early warning systems, we can help mitigate the risk of political instability and conflict.
- **Digital diplomacy**: Social media and other digital communication platforms can facilitate dialogue between governments, organizations, and individuals, promoting understanding and cooperation on a global scale. By leveraging these technologies for diplomacy, we can help build bridges and prevent conflicts from escalating.
- **Peacebuilding apps**: Mobile applications, such as PeaceApp, Build Up, and Soliya, can be used to connect people from diverse backgrounds, provide conflict resolution training, and foster cross-cultural understanding. By adopting and promoting these peacebuilding apps, we can contribute to a more peaceful and inclusive world.

- **Virtual reality (VR) for empathy-building**: VR experiences can transport users to conflict zones, refugee camps, and other challenging environments, helping to build empathy and understanding. By supporting the development and use of these immersive technologies, we can help raise awareness about the realities of political instability and conflict, fostering a greater sense of global responsibility.
- **Crowdsourcing and citizen journalism**: Platforms like Ushahidi and Global Voices enable people in conflict-affected areas to share their stories and experiences, providing real-time insights into political instability and violence. By supporting these platforms and amplifying the voices of those affected by

conflict, we can help create a more informed and engaged global community.

Raising Awareness and Taking Action

As with other issues we've discussed in this book, raising awareness about political instability and conflict is crucial. Share information about the challenges and opportunities related to these issues, as well as the innovative technologies available to help address them, with your friends, family, and colleagues. Engage in conversations, attend local events, and join advocacy groups to stay informed and involved.

By raising awareness and taking small actions, you can contribute to the global effort to promote peace and stability. In the next chapter of "Giving a F*ck," *we'll explore another pressing issue and discuss how we can work together to create positive change. Keep learning, keep sharing, and never stop giving a f*ck*! Together, we can make a meaningful impact and build a more peaceful and harmonious world for all.

Chapter 11: Terrorism and Extremism - Building Bridges and Promoting Tolerance

Welcome back to "Giving a F*ck"! So far, we've tackled a range of pressing global issues, including climate change, poverty, inequality, global health, food and water insecurity, forced migration and refugee crises, access to education, gender inequality, environmental degradation, and political instability and conflict. In this chapter, we'll delve into terrorism and extremism, shedding light on the impacts of these issues and exploring ways to address them.

Terrorism and extremism pose significant threats to global security and stability. These issues can manifest in various forms, such as religious, political, or ideological extremism, and often result in violence, fear, and societal division. To better understand the scope of terrorism and extremism, let's look at some key statistics:

- The Global Terrorism Index (GTI) reported a total of 13,826 terrorist incidents in 2019, resulting in 13,826 deaths.
- According to the same report, the economic impact of terrorism was estimated at $26.4 billion in 2019.
- A study by the United Nations Office of Counter-Terrorism (UNOCT) found that, as of 2020, there were more than 160,000 foreign terrorist fighters from over 110 countries.

These statistics underscore the severity and global reach of terrorism and extremism. But there's hope – by working together, we can help prevent and mitigate the impacts of these issues. Let's explore some small steps you can take to make a difference.

Small Steps to Make a Difference

- **Stay informed and educate others**: Keep up to date with current events, learn about the root causes of terrorism and extremism, and share this information with others. By promoting understanding and awareness, you can help foster empathy and encourage peaceful resolution of conflicts.

- **Support counter-terrorism and counter-extremism organizations**: Numerous organizations, such as the Institute for Strategic Dialogue, the International Centre for Counter-Terrorism, and the Global Community Engagement and Resilience Fund, work to prevent, mitigate, and respond to terrorism and extremism. By donating to, volunteering for, or advocating on behalf of these organizations, you can help support their vital work.
- **Engage in dialogue and promote tolerance**: Encourage open, respectful conversations with others who hold different views or come from different backgrounds. By fostering dialogue and promoting tolerance, you can help bridge divides and contribute to a more peaceful and inclusive society.
- **Report suspicious activity**: If you see something that seems suspicious or potentially related to terrorism or extremism, report it to your local law enforcement or the appropriate authorities. By remaining vigilant and reporting concerns, you can help keep your community safe.

Now that we've covered some personal actions, let's take a look at some of the innovative technologies that are helping to address terrorism and extremism worldwide.

Technologies to Address Terrorism and Extremism

- **Advanced surveillance and monitoring**: Cutting-edge surveillance systems, biometrics, and facial recognition technologies can help authorities identify and track potential terrorists and extremists. By supporting the development and implementation of these technologies, we can help enhance global security and prevent terrorist attacks.

- **Artificial intelligence (AI) for threat detection**: AI algorithms can analyze large volumes of data from social media, online forums, and other sources to identify potential threats, extremist content, and patterns of radicalization. By supporting the development and use of AI for threat detection, we can help to identify and counteract terrorism and extremism more effectively.
- **Counter-extremism messaging and online platforms**: Digital platforms and social media campaigns can help to counteract extremist propaganda and promote alternative narratives that foster peace, understanding, and tolerance. Initiatives such as Google's Redirect Method and Facebook's Counter Speech Program use targeted advertising and counter-narratives to dissuade individuals from engaging with extremist content. By supporting these initiatives and sharing their messages, you can contribute to the fight against online radicalization.

- **Crowdsourcing intelligence**: Platforms like See Something, Send Something and Terrorist Reporting App allow citizens to report suspicious activities or information related to terrorism and extremism directly to law enforcement agencies. By adopting and promoting these technologies, we can foster a more vigilant and engaged society that works together to combat terrorism and extremism.
- **Virtual reality (VR) for empathy-building and training**: VR experiences can be used to create immersive simulations that help people understand the perspectives of those affected by terrorism and extremism. Additionally, VR can be used to train law enforcement and counter-terrorism personnel in effective response and de-escalation tactics. By supporting the development and use of VR for these purposes, we can promote

empathy and improve our collective ability to address terrorism and extremism.

Raising Awareness and Taking Action

As with other issues we've discussed in this book, raising awareness about terrorism and extremism is essential. Share information about the challenges and opportunities related to these issues, as well as the innovative technologies available to help address them, with your friends, family, and colleagues. Engage in conversations, attend local events, and join advocacy groups to stay informed and involved.

By raising awareness and taking small actions, you can contribute to the global effort to prevent and mitigate the impacts of terrorism and extremism. In the next chapter of "Giving a F*ck," *we'll explore another pressing issue and discuss how we can work together to create positive change. Keep learning, keep sharing, and never stop giving a f*ck*! Together, we can make a meaningful impact and build a more peaceful and harmonious world for all.

Chapter 12: Cybersecurity and Data Privacy - Safeguarding Our Digital Lives

Welcome back to "Giving a F*ck"! Throughout this book, we've been discussing pressing global issues and exploring the small steps we can take to make a difference. In this chapter, we'll focus on cybersecurity and data privacy, two interconnected concerns that affect our increasingly digital lives.

The digital age has transformed the way we live, work, and connect with others. However, as we increasingly rely on technology, we also face new risks related to cybersecurity and data privacy. Cyberattacks, data breaches, and online surveillance can have serious implications for individuals, organizations, and even governments. Let's examine some key statistics to understand the scale of these issues:

- According to Cybersecurity Ventures, global cybercrime costs are expected to reach $10.5 trillion annually by 2025, up from $3 trillion in 2015.
- In 2021, the Identity Theft Resource Center reported a 17% increase in the number of data breaches compared to the previous year.
- A study by the Pew Research Center found that 64% of Americans have experienced a data breach, and 49% feel their personal information is less secure than it was five years ago.

These statistics highlight the growing challenges associated with cybersecurity and data privacy. But fear not – by working together and taking proactive steps, we can help protect ourselves and our digital communities. Let's explore some small steps you can take to make a difference.

Small Steps to Make a Difference

- **Strengthen your passwords**: Use strong, unique passwords for each of your online accounts, and consider using a password manager to help you remember them. A strong password should include a mix of upper and lower case letters, numbers, and symbols.
- **Enable two-factor authentication (2FA)**: 2FA adds an extra layer of security to your accounts by requiring you to verify your identity with a second factor, such as a text message or biometric data. Enable 2FA wherever possible to reduce the risk of unauthorized access to your accounts.
- **Keep your devices and software up to date**: Regularly update your devices, operating systems, and applications to protect against known vulnerabilities and security threats.
- **Be cautious with public Wi-Fi**: Avoid using public Wi-Fi networks for sensitive activities, such as online banking or accessing confidential information. If you must use public Wi-Fi, use a virtual private network (VPN) to encrypt your connection and protect your data.
- **Stay informed and educate others**: Keep up to date with the latest cybersecurity threats and best practices, and share this information with friends, family, and colleagues. By promoting awareness and fostering a culture of cybersecurity, you can help protect your digital community.

Now that we've covered some personal actions, let's take a look at some of the innovative technologies that are helping to address cybersecurity and data privacy worldwide.

Technologies to Address Cybersecurity and Data Privacy

- **Artificial intelligence (AI) and machine learning**: AI and machine learning algorithms can analyze vast amounts of data to detect suspicious activity, identify potential threats, and respond to cyberattacks in real-time. By supporting the development and adoption of these technologies, we can help to enhance cybersecurity and protect our digital lives.

- **Blockchain technology**: Blockchain's decentralized and transparent nature can help improve data privacy and security by making it more difficult for hackers to tamper with or gain unauthorized access to sensitive information. By promoting and adopting blockchain-based solutions, we can contribute to a more secure digital ecosystem.
- **End-to-end encryption (E2EE)**: E2EE ensures that only the sender and the intended recipient can access the content of a message or communication, as it is encrypted on the sender's device and only decrypted on the recipient's device. By using and promoting E2EE messaging apps and services, such as Signal or WhatsApp, we can help safeguard our privacy and protect our communications from eavesdropping and surveillance.

- **Privacy-enhancing technologies (PETs)**: PETs, such as zero-knowledge proofs, homomorphic encryption, and secure multi-party computation, allow users to share and process data without revealing the underlying information. By supporting the development and adoption of PETs, we can strike a balance between data utility and privacy, enabling new opportunities for secure data sharing and collaboration.
- **Cybersecurity awareness training**: Educational platforms like KnowBe4, Infosec, and Cybrary offer online training and resources designed to teach individuals and organizations about cybersecurity best practices, threat identification, and incident response. By investing in cybersecurity education and training, we can empower ourselves and others to stay safe in the digital

world.

Raising Awareness and Taking Action

As with other issues we've discussed in this book, raising awareness about cybersecurity and data privacy is crucial. Share information about the challenges and opportunities related to these issues, as well as the innovative technologies available to help address them, with your friends, family, and colleagues. Engage in conversations, attend local events, and join advocacy groups to stay informed and involved.

By raising awareness and taking small actions, you can contribute to the global effort to enhance cybersecurity and protect data privacy. In the next chapter of "Giving a F*ck," *we'll explore another pressing issue and discuss how we can work together to create positive change. Keep learning, keep sharing, and never stop giving a f*ck*! Together, we can make a meaningful impact and build a safer and more secure digital world for all.

Bonus Chapter: Entrepreneurs & Business Leaders - Getting Involved

Dear reader, congratulations on reaching the bonus chapter! In this section, we'll explore how entrepreneurs and business leaders can play a crucial role in addressing the world's most pressing problems. Companies and business leaders have the power, resources, and influence to drive significant change, and as the world faces increasing challenges, now is the time to step up and contribute to the global effort.

Throughout this book, we've discussed various global problems, such as climate change, poverty, inequality, global health issues, and more. While these issues may seem daunting, they also present opportunities for innovative entrepreneurs and business leaders to create new solutions and make a real impact. Let's explore how businesses can seize these opportunities and contribute to solving some of these pressing problems.

- **Climate Change**

Climate change is one of the most significant threats we face today. To mitigate its impact, businesses can develop and invest in clean and renewable energy solutions, green technologies, and sustainable products. They can also implement environmentally friendly policies and practices within their operations, such as reducing waste, conserving energy, and promoting recycling.

Statistics show that the global clean energy market was valued at $928.0 billion in 2017 and is projected to reach $1,512.3 billion by 2025, growing at a CAGR of 6.1% from 2018 to 2025. This presents a vast opportunity for businesses to enter the clean energy sector and contribute to the global transition towards renewable energy sources.

- **Poverty**

Businesses can play a critical role in addressing poverty by creating jobs, providing fair wages, and promoting economic growth in impoverished regions. They can invest in local communities, support small businesses, and foster entrepreneurship by providing training, mentorship, and financial assistance.

In addition, businesses can develop innovative products and services that cater to the needs of the poor, such as affordable housing, clean water solutions, and accessible healthcare. The World Bank estimates that the market for goods and services targeting low-income consumers is worth $5 trillion, offering significant opportunities for businesses to create social impact while also generating profits.

- **Inequality**

To tackle inequality, businesses can implement policies that promote diversity, inclusion, and equal opportunities for all employees, regardless of their gender, race, or socioeconomic background. They can also provide equal pay for equal work, invest in education and training programs, and offer mentorship and career development opportunities to underrepresented groups.

Supporting fair trade practices, paying living wages to suppliers, and partnering with organizations that work to reduce inequality are other ways businesses can contribute to closing the income gap. The Global Impact Investing Network (GIIN) reports that impact investing assets under management reached $715 billion in 2020, signalling growing interest in businesses that seek to address social and environmental issues.

- **Global Health Issues**

Entrepreneurs and business leaders can help address global health issues by investing in research and development of innovative healthcare solutions, such as new drugs, medical devices, and digital health technologies. They can also promote access to affordable healthcare by developing low-cost products and services tailored to the needs of underserved populations.

Moreover, businesses can support public health initiatives, promote healthy lifestyles among employees, and contribute to building healthcare infrastructure in underdeveloped regions. The global digital health market is expected to reach $504.4 billion by 2025, growing at a CAGR of 29.6% from 2018 to 2025, offering significant opportunities for businesses to make a difference in global health.

- **Food and Water Insecurity**

Businesses can contribute to solving food and water insecurity by investing in innovative agricultural technologies, sustainable farming practices, and efficient water management systems. They can also support efforts to reduce food waste, improve food distribution networks, and develop nutritious, affordable food products for low-income consumers.

Companies can collaborate with NGOs and government agencies to implement water conservation and sanitation projects in vulnerable communities. According to a report by the Food and Agriculture Organization of the United Nations, the global agri-food sector offers a $2.3 trillion market opportunity for businesses that address food and water insecurity challenges.

- **Forced Migration and Refugee Crises**

Entrepreneurs and business leaders can help address the forced migration and refugee crises by providing employment opportunities, skills training, and support for social integration to displaced people. They can also invest in businesses that cater to the unique needs of refugees, such as affordable housing, language training, and healthcare services.

Collaborating with NGOs and government agencies to develop innovative solutions for refugee settlements and supporting advocacy campaigns to raise awareness about the issue are other ways businesses can contribute to addressing this global challenge. The global humanitarian aid market was valued at $27.3 billion in 2019, highlighting the potential for businesses to create innovative solutions for displaced populations.

- **Access to Education**

Investing in education is crucial for creating a more equitable and prosperous world. Businesses can contribute to improving access to quality education by supporting initiatives such as scholarship programs, mentorship, and training opportunities for underprivileged students. They can also invest in edtech startups and develop innovative educational tools and platforms that make learning more accessible and engaging for students around the world.

By partnering with NGOs and educational institutions, businesses can help address the global education gap and create a skilled workforce for the future. The global edtech market is expected to reach $404 billion by 2025, presenting significant opportunities for businesses to contribute to educational advancement.

- **Gender Inequality**

Tackling gender inequality requires businesses to promote diversity and inclusion in the workplace, providing equal opportunities for men and women to advance their careers. They can also invest in female-owned businesses, support women's entrepreneurship, and promote gender-sensitive policies and practices throughout their supply chains.

Additionally, businesses can collaborate with NGOs and government agencies to support initiatives that empower women, such as education, healthcare, and legal rights programs. The global gender-lens investing market reached $4.8 billion in assets under management in 2020, indicating the growing interest in businesses that address gender inequality.

- **Environmental Degradation**

Entrepreneurs and business leaders can help combat environmental degradation by developing sustainable products and services, adopting eco-friendly business practices, and investing in technologies that promote conservation and restoration of natural resources. They can also support reforestation projects, biodiversity conservation initiatives, and campaigns to raise awareness about the importance of preserving our planet.

Businesses that embrace circular economy principles and focus on reducing waste, recycling, and upcycling can also contribute to addressing environmental degradation. The global market for environmental technologies is projected to reach $1.2 trillion by 2025, offering ample opportunities for businesses to make a positive impact.

- **Political Instability and Conflict**

Businesses can play a role in promoting peace and stability by investing in conflict-affected regions, supporting community development programs, and creating jobs that help rebuild local economies. They can also advocate for responsible business practices and policies that foster peace, security, and inclusive growth.

Partnering with NGOs, government agencies, and other stakeholders to support peacebuilding initiatives and address the root causes of conflict can further contribute to global stability. The peace and security market, which includes industries such as cybersecurity, defense, and peacekeeping, is estimated to be worth over $500 billion annually, presenting opportunities for businesses to get involved.

In conclusion, entrepreneurs and business leaders have the power to make a significant impact on the world's most pressing problems. By identifying opportunities, embracing innovation, and leveraging their resources and influence, they can drive positive change and create a better future for all. So, let's encourage the business community to step up, take action, and make a difference. As a reader of this book, you can contribute by supporting companies that are actively addressing these global issues, advocating for responsible business practices, and spreading awareness about the role businesses can play in solving world problems.

Remember that change starts with individuals, and by choosing to "give a f*ck" about one or more of these pressing issues, you're already making a difference. As you continue on your journey, keep learning, keep growing, and keep challenging yourself and others to make the world a better place.

Together, we can create a more equitable, sustainable, and prosperous future for all. Let's give a f*ck and make it happen!

Bonus Chapter: Impact Investors - Getting Involved

Hey there, reader! If you've made it this far, you're already showing that you genuinely give a f*ck about the world we live in and the many problems it faces. In this bonus chapter, we'll be focusing on a powerful group of individuals who can make a significant impact: impact investors. We'll discuss what impact investment is, how it can help businesses offering solutions to the world problems mentioned earlier, and how businesses can access impact investments. Let's dive in!

What is Impact Investment?

Impact investment is an approach to investment that focuses on generating positive social and environmental impact alongside financial returns. This means that impact investors are not only concerned with making money but also with making a meaningful, measurable difference in the world. Impact investments can span various asset classes, such as public and private equity, fixed income, and real assets. They also cover a wide range of sectors, including renewable energy, sustainable agriculture, education, healthcare, affordable housing, and more.

How can impact investors help businesses offering solutions to world problems?

- **Providing capital**: Many businesses working on innovative solutions to global issues require capital to scale up, expand their operations, or develop new technologies. Impact investors can help by providing much-needed funding to these businesses in the form of equity investments, loans, or grants.
- **Encouraging innovation**: Impact investors often support businesses that are pushing the boundaries of traditional industries, developing new technologies, or disrupting existing markets. By investing in these innovative ventures, impact

investors can help accelerate the development and adoption of solutions to the world's most pressing problems.

- **Sharing expertise**: Many impact investors have backgrounds in entrepreneurship, finance, or specific sectors relevant to the global issues they seek to address. By partnering with businesses working on these problems, impact investors can share their knowledge, experience, and connections to help these companies grow and succeed.
- **Attracting additional investment**: When impact investors back a business, they can help attract further investment from other sources, such as venture capitalists, angel investors, or government grants. This additional funding can be crucial for businesses trying to scale their operations or reach new markets.
- **Raising awareness**: Impact investors can play a significant role in raising awareness about the businesses they support and the global issues these companies are tackling. By promoting their investments and sharing their stories, impact investors can inspire others to take action and support similar ventures.

How can businesses access impact investments?

- **Develop a clear social or environmental impact thesis**: To attract impact investors, businesses need to demonstrate how their products or services create a positive impact on society or the environment. Develop a clear and compelling narrative that outlines your impact goals, the specific problem you are addressing, and how your business model contributes to solving that problem.
- **Measure and report impact**: Impact investors want to see evidence of the social and environmental outcomes generated by the businesses they support. Develop a system for measuring and reporting your impact, using standardized metrics like the

Global Impact Investing Network's (GIIN) IRIS+ framework, where possible.

- **Network and engage**: Attend conferences, events, and workshops focused on impact investing or your specific sector. Use these opportunities to network with potential investors, learn about new trends and opportunities, and showcase your business.
- **Research and target potential investors**: Impact investors have varying investment preferences and sector focuses. Research potential investors and identify those whose interests align with your business and impact goals. Create a targeted list of investors and develop a tailored approach for engaging with them.
- **Build a strong team and advisory board**: Impact investors look for businesses with a strong management team and an experienced advisory board. Assemble a diverse team with complementary skills and backgrounds and consider adding advisors with industry expertise, connections, or experience in impact investing.

In conclusion, impact investors have the potential to play a crucial role in addressing the world's most pressing problems. By providing capital, encouraging innovation, sharing expertise, attracting additional investment, and raising awareness, impact investors can help businesses develop and scale solutions to tackle these challenges.

As an entrepreneur or business leader, it's essential to understand the value of impact investment and how it can help your venture grow while creating positive change. By developing a clear impact thesis, measuring and reporting your impact, networking and engaging with potential investors, and building a strong team and advisory board, you can position your business to attract the attention and support of impact investors.

And for those of you who are impact investors or are considering becoming one, remember that your investments can make a significant difference in the world. By supporting businesses that address the world's most pressing problems, you can not only generate financial returns but also help create a more sustainable, equitable, and just future for all.

Now that you've learned about the many ways you can give a f*ck about the world's problems, it's time to take action. Whether you're an individual, entrepreneur, business leader, or impact investor, every small step counts. We hope that this book has inspired you to choose one or more issues close to your heart and make a positive impact through your actions, technology adoption, or investments.

Together, we can create a better world for ourselves and future generations. So, let's start giving a f*ck and making a difference today!

Final Chapter: Thank You and A Call to Action

Dear reader, as we reach the final chapter of "Giving a F*ck," we want to extend our sincerest gratitude for joining us on this journey. Throughout the book, we've explored some of the most pressing world problems and discussed the small steps we can take to address them. We've also looked at innovative technologies that can help us tackle these challenges and create a better world for all.

Now, it's time for a call to action. While reading this book, you've likely felt a connection to one or more of the issues we've discussed. Whether it's climate change, inequality, global health, or any of the other challenges we've examined, we urge you to take action and make a difference. Your individual efforts may seem small, but collectively, we can bring about significant change.

Here's how you can start:

- **Choose your cause**: Reflect on the issues we've covered in this book and identify the one(s) that resonate with you the most. It's important to select a cause that you're passionate about, as it will drive you to take meaningful action and stay committed in the long run.
- **Raise awareness**: Share what you've learned with friends, family, and colleagues. Start conversations about the issue(s) you've chosen, and encourage others to join the discussion. By raising awareness, we can inspire collective action and bring more attention to the problems we're trying to solve.
- **Leverage technology**: Harness the power of technology to amplify your impact. Utilize the tools and platforms we've mentioned in this book to educate yourself further, connect with like-minded individuals, and take action. Remember, the

technologies available today can help us address global challenges more effectively and efficiently than ever before.

- **Support organizations and initiatives**: Many organizations and initiatives are already working to address the world's most pressing problems. Research and support those that align with your chosen cause, either by volunteering your time, donating resources, or sharing their message. Together, we can amplify their impact.
- **Continue learning and growing**: Stay informed about the latest developments in your chosen issue(s), and remain open to new ideas and perspectives. As you learn more, you'll be better equipped to make a difference and adapt your efforts to the ever-changing landscape of global challenges.
- **Be patient and persistent**: Making a difference in the world takes time, effort, and determination. Don't be disheartened if you don't see immediate results. Instead, celebrate small victories and stay committed to your cause, knowing that your efforts are contributing to a larger, collective impact.

Remember, each one of us has the power to make a difference. By choosing a cause, raising awareness, leveraging technology, and taking definitive action, you're not only giving a f*ck, but you're also playing an essential role in creating a better world for future generations.

As we conclude this book, we want to leave you with a few final thoughts and encouragements. The journey of giving a f*ck and making a difference is not always an easy one, but it is undoubtedly a rewarding and fulfilling path.

Stay connected: Building a supportive network of like-minded individuals is essential for sustained activism and engagement. Join online communities, attend local events, and participate in discussions related to your chosen cause. By staying connected, you'll gain valuable insights, encouragement, and resources that can help you maintain your momentum and maximize your impact.

Be adaptable and open to change: The world is constantly evolving, and so are the challenges we face. Be prepared to adapt your approach and embrace change as new information and technologies become available. Keep an open mind and be willing to revise your strategies and tactics to stay effective in your efforts to create a better world.

Practice self-care: While giving a f*ck about the world and working towards positive change is important, it's also essential to take care of yourself. Remember that self-care is not selfish – it's necessary for your well-being and long-term effectiveness. Make time for rest, relaxation, and personal growth to ensure that you can continue to give your best to the causes you care about.

Celebrate progress: Finally, always remember to celebrate the progress that you and others are making. Acknowledge the achievements, no matter how small, and take pride in the knowledge that your actions are contributing to positive change. Celebrating progress helps to maintain motivation and reminds us that our efforts are not in vain.

Thank you once more for joining us on this journey and for choosing to give a f*ck about the world and its challenges. You are part of a global community of changemakers who, together, are working towards a brighter and more just future. We hope that this book has inspired you, empowered you, and given you the tools to take action in a meaningful and effective way.

As you continue on your path, remember to be patient, persistent, and compassionate – not only towards others but also towards yourself. And most importantly, never stop giving a f*ck. Your passion, dedication, and actions are what will ultimately make the world a better place.

With our warmest wishes for your continued success and impact,

Somdip Dey, FRSA,

The author of "Giving a F*ck"

• • • •

Connect With The Author

Hope the contents from this book have helped you to gain fundamental understanding of some of the pressing issues in the world and raise awareness on them. I often post related contents on sustainability development on my social media channels as follows:

LinkedIn: http://linkedin.com/in/somdipdey

Facebook: http://facebook.com/deysomdip

Koo: http://kooapp.com/profile/somdipdey

Let's stay in touch and help each other to build a better world!

www.ingramcontent.com/pod-product-compliance
Ingram Content Group UK Ltd.
Pitfield, Milton Keynes, MK11 3LW, UK
UKHW042012190726
13854UKWH00005B/2255